This Book Belongs to:

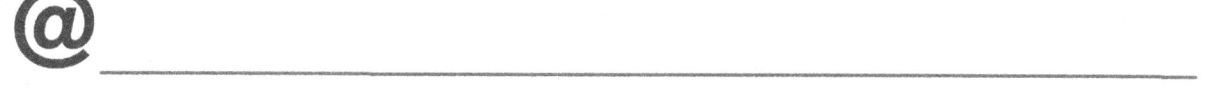

$500 CHALLENGE IN 26 WEEKS

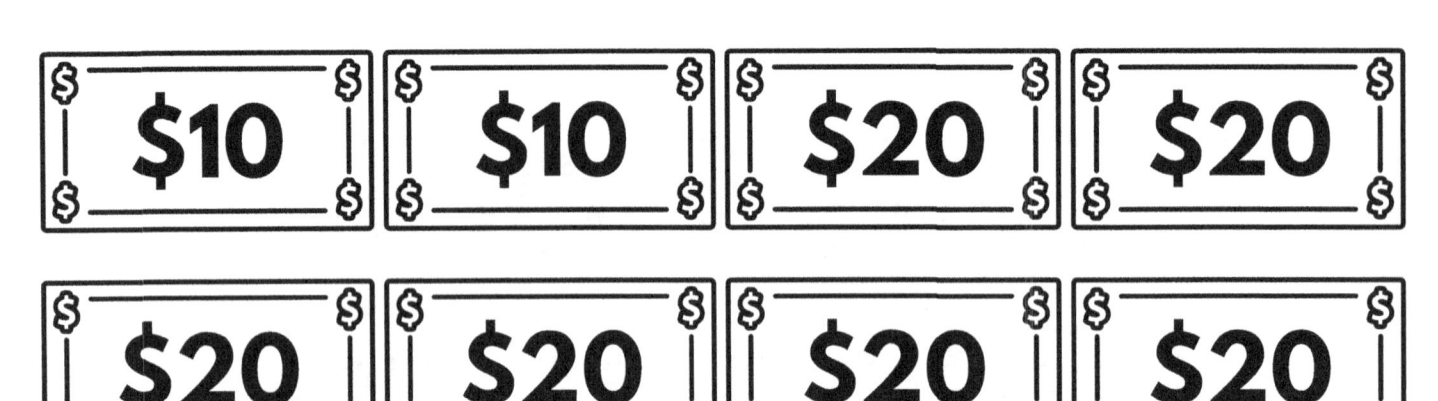

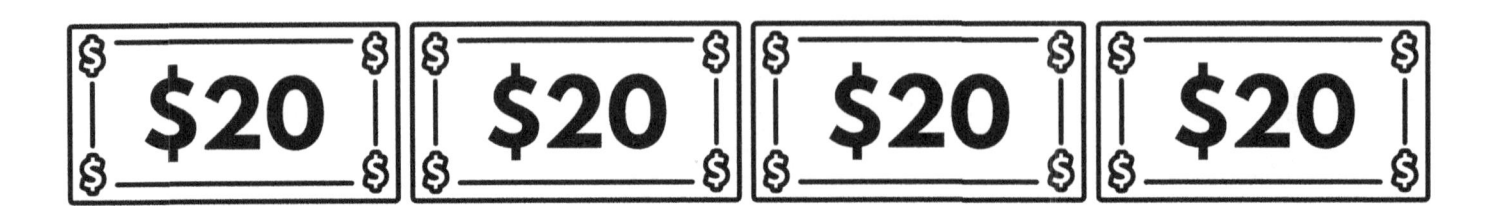

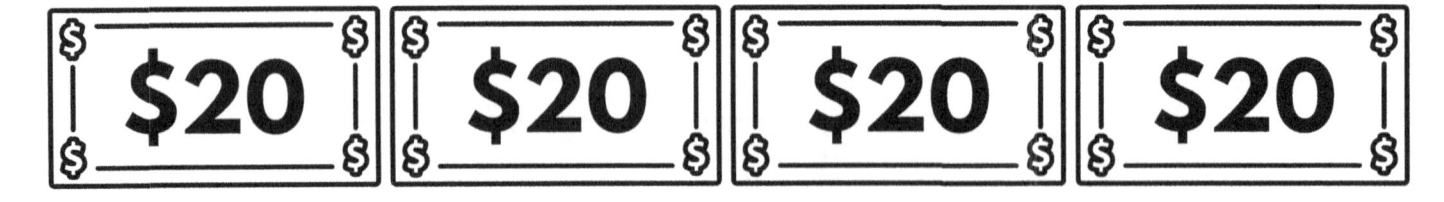

Saving Purpose: _____

$10	$10	$20	$20
$20	$20	$20	$20
$20	$20	$20	$20
$20	$20	$20	$20
$20	$20	$20	$20
$20	$20	$20	$20

$20 $20   = $500

$500 CHALLENGE IN 26 WEEKS

Saving Purpose: _____

$10	$10	$20	$20
$20	$20	$20	$20
$20	$20	$20	$20
$20	$20	$20	$20
$20	$20	$20	$20
$20	$20	$20	$20

$20 $20 = $500

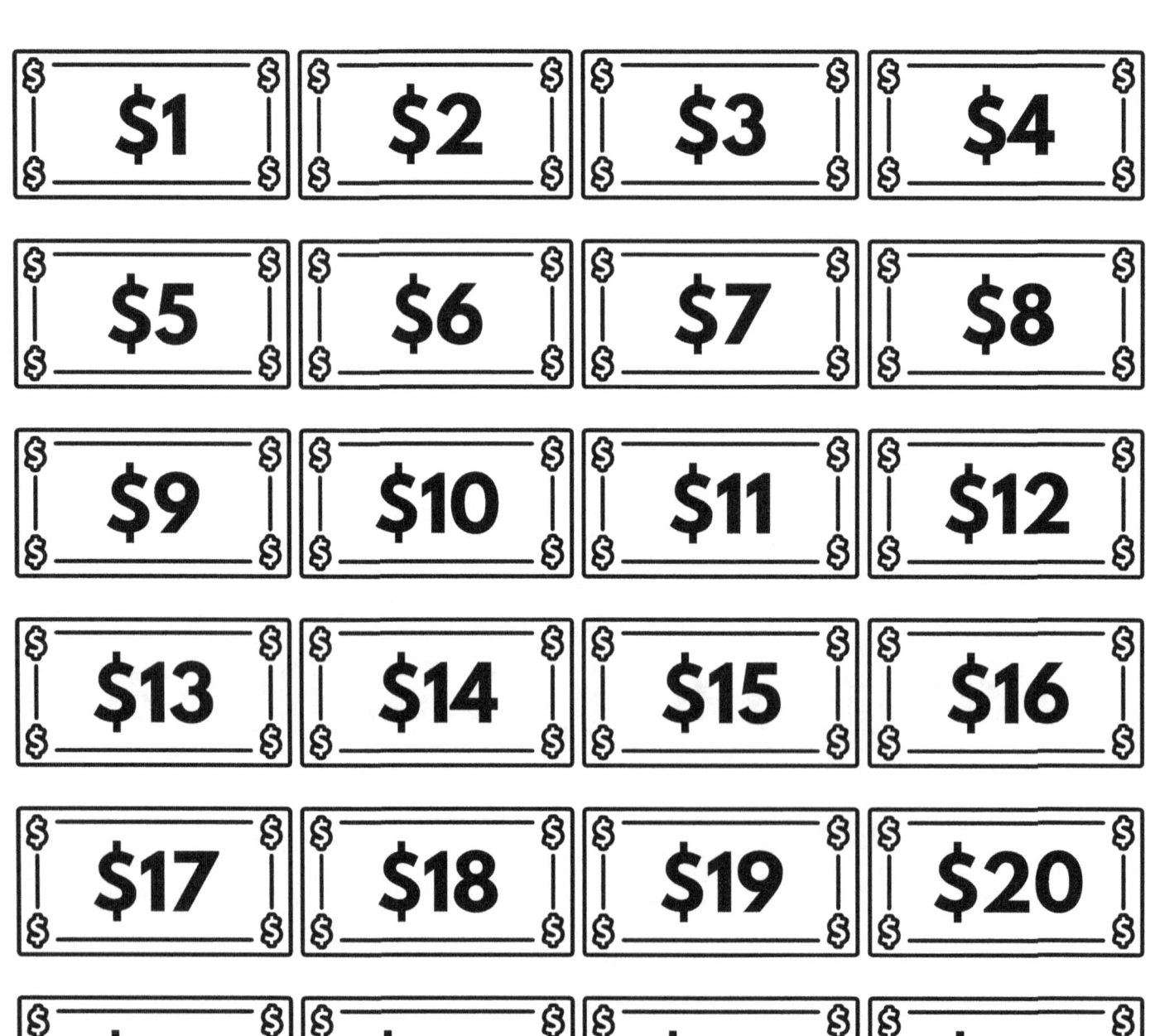

$700 CHALLENGE IN 26 WEEKS

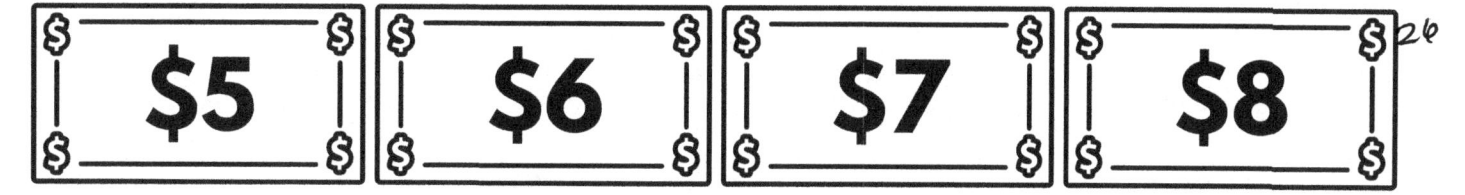

Saving Purpose: _____

$1	$2	$3	$4	10
$5	$6	$7	$8	26
$9	$10	$11	$12	42
$13	$14	$15	$16	58
$17	$18	$19	$20	74
$21	$22	$23	$24	90
$25	$26			51

= $700

$1,000 CHALLENGE IN 26 WEEKS

Saving Purpose: _____

$20	$20	$40	$40
$40	$40	$40	$40
$40	$40	$40	$40
$40	$40	$40	$40
$40	$40	$40	$40
$40	$40	$40	$40

$40 $40 = **$1,000**

$1,000 CHALLENGE IN 26 WEEKS

Saving Purpose: _____

$10	$15	$20	$20
$20	$25	$25	$25
$30	$30	$35	$35
$40	$40	$45	$45
$45	$50	$50	$50
$55	$55	$55	$60

| $60 | $60 | = **$1,000** |

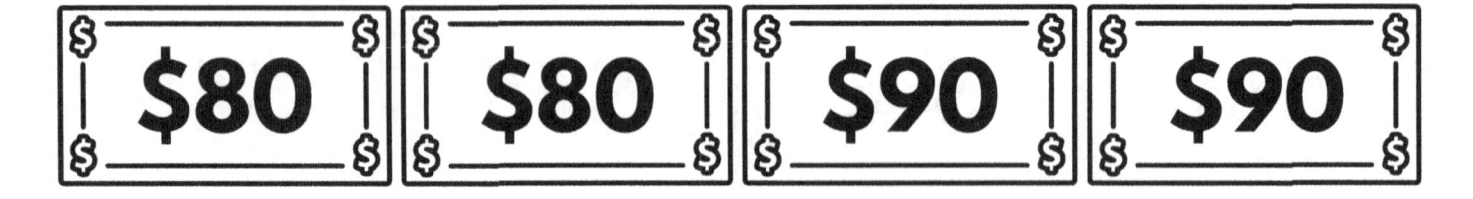

$2,000 CHALLENGE IN 26 WEEKS

Saving Purpose: _____

$20	$30	$40	$40
$40	$50	$50	$50
$60	$60	$70	$70
$80	$80	$90	$90
$90	$100	$100	$100
$110	$110	$110	$120

$120 $120 = $2,000

$2,000 CHALLENGE IN 26 WEEKS

Saving Purpose: _____

$75	$75	$75	$75
$75	$75	$75	$75
$75	$75	$75	$75
$75	$75	$75	$75
$80	$80	$80	$80
$80	$80	$80	$80
$80	$80	= **$2,000**

$3,000 CHALLENGE IN 26 WEEKS

Saving Purpose: _____

$75	$75	$75	$75
$75	$75	$100	$100
$100	$100	$100	$100
$125	$125	$125	$125
$125	$125	$150	$150
$150	$150	$150	$150
$150	$150	= $3,000

$3,000 CHALLENGE IN 26 WEEKS

Saving Purpose: _____

$115	$115	$115	$115
$115	$115	$115	$115
$115	$115	$115	$115
$115	$115	$115	$115
$115	$115	$115	$115
$115	$115	$115	$115

$120 $120 = $3,000

$4,000 CHALLENGE IN 26 WEEKS

Saving Purpose: _____

$100	$110	$120	$130
$140	$150	$150	$150
$150	$150	$150	$150
$150	$150	$150	$150
$150	$160	$160	$170
$170	$180	$180	$190

$190 $200 = $4,000

$4,000 CHALLENGE IN 26 WEEKS

Saving Purpose: _____

$150	$150	$150	$150
$150	$150	$155	$155
$155	$155	$155	$155
$155	$155	$155	$155
$155	$155	$155	$155
$155	$155	$155	$155

$155 $155 = **$4,000**

$5,000 CHALLENGE IN 26 WEEKS

Saving Purpose: _____

$55	$65	$75	$85
$95	$100	$105	$125
$125	$150	$160	$175
$185	$190	$200	$225
$235	$240	$250	$275
$275	$300	$315	$320

$325 | $350 = **$5,000**

$5,000 CHALLENGE IN 26 WEEKS

Saving Purpose: _____

$190	$190	$190	$190
$190	$190	$190	$190
$190	$190	$190	$190
$190	$190	$195	$195
$195	$195	$195	$195
$195	$195	$195	$195

$195 $195 = **$5,000**

$10,000 CHALLENGE IN 26 WEEKS

Saving Purpose: _____

$90	$180	$190	$210
$270	$295	$330	$350
$350	$360	$365	$385
$385	$400	$425	$435
$450	$460	$480	$490
$500	$500	$510	$510
$525	$555	= $10,000

$10,000 CHALLENGE IN 26 WEEKS

Saving Purpose: _____

$380	$380	$385	$385
$385	$385	$385	$385
$385	$385	$385	$385
$385	$385	$385	$385
$385	$385	$385	$385
$385	$385	$385	$385

$385 $385 = $10,000

$15,000 CHALLENGE IN 26 WEEKS

Saving Purpose: _____

$460	$470	$480	$490
$500	$500	$510	$520
$530	$540	$550	$560
$570	$580	$590	$600
$610	$620	$630	$640
$650	$660	$670	$680

$690 $700 = **$15,000**

$15,000 CHALLENGE IN 26 WEEKS

Saving Purpose: _____

$460	$470	$480	$490
$500	$500	$510	$520
$530	$540	$550	$560
$570	$580	$590	$600
$610	$620	$630	$640
$650	$660	$670	$680
$690	$700

= $15,000

CUSTOM CHALLENGE IN 26 WEEKS

Saving Purpose: _____

Total: _____

CUSTOM CHALLENGE IN 26 WEEKS

Saving Purpose: _____

Total: _____

$500 CHALLENGE IN 26 WEEKS

Saving Purpose: _____

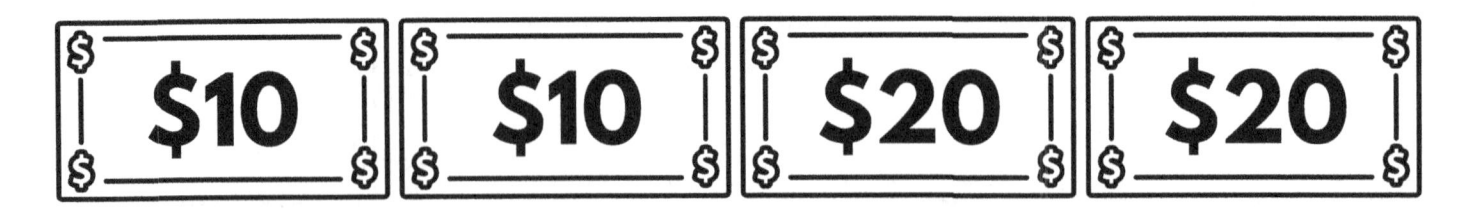

$10	$10	$20	$20
$20	$20	$20	$20
$20	$20	$20	$20
$20	$20	$20	$20
$20	$20	$20	$20
$20	$20	$20	$20

$20 $20 = $500

$500 CHALLENGE IN 26 WEEKS

Saving Purpose: _____

$10	$10	$20	$20
$20	$20	$20	$20
$20	$20	$20	$20
$20	$20	$20	$20
$20	$20	$20	$20
$20	$20	$20	$20

$20 $20 **= $500**

$700 CHALLENGE IN 26 WEEKS

Saving Purpose: _____

$1	$2	$3	$4
$5	$6	$7	$8
$9	$10	$11	$12
$13	$14	$15	$16
$17	$18	$19	$20
$21	$22	$23	$24
$25	$26

= **$700**

$700 CHALLENGE IN 26 WEEKS

Saving Purpose: _____

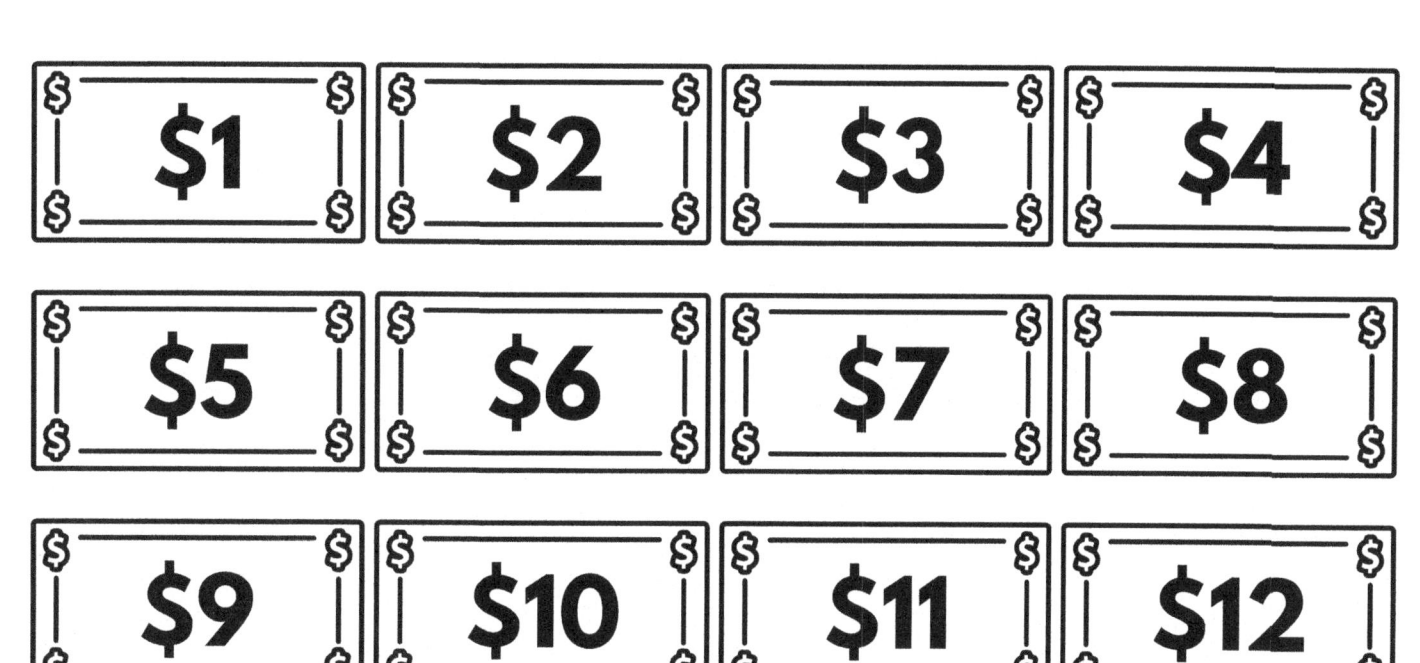

$1	$2	$3	$4
$5	$6	$7	$8
$9	$10	$11	$12
$13	$14	$15	$16
$17	$18	$19	$20
$21	$22	$23	$24

$25 $26   **= $700**

$1,000 CHALLENGE IN 26 WEEKS

Saving Purpose: _____

$20	$20	$40	$40
$40	$40	$40	$40
$40	$40	$40	$40
$40	$40	$40	$40
$40	$40	$40	$40
$40	$40	$40	$40

$40 $40 = **$1,000**

$1,000 CHALLENGE IN 26 WEEKS

Saving Purpose: _____

$10	$15	$20	$20
$20	$25	$25	$25
$30	$30	$35	$35
$40	$40	$45	$45
$45	$50	$50	$50
$55	$55	$55	$60
$60	$60

= **$1,000**

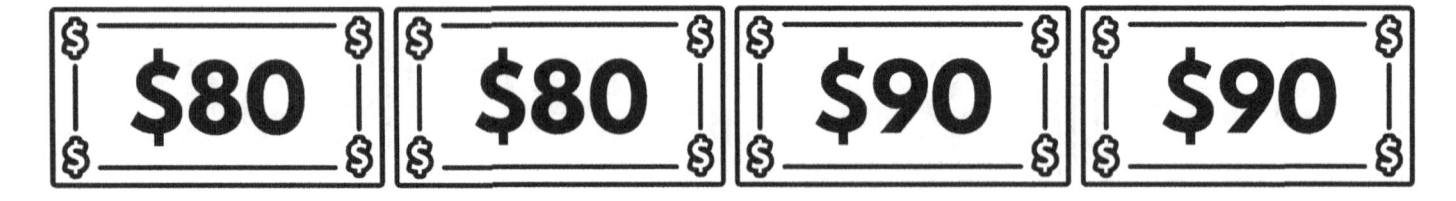

$2,000 CHALLENGE IN 26 WEEKS

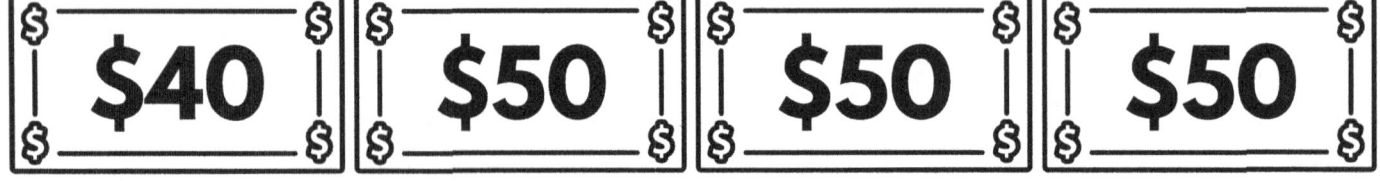

Saving Purpose: _____

$20	$30	$40	$40
$40	$50	$50	$50
$60	$60	$70	$70
$80	$80	$90	$90
$90	$100	$100	$100
$110	$110	$110	$120

$120 $120 = **$2,000**

$2,000 CHALLENGE IN 26 WEEKS

Saving Purpose: _____

$75	$75	$75	$75
$75	$75	$75	$75
$75	$75	$75	$75
$75	$75	$75	$75
$80	$80	$80	$80
$80	$80	$80	$80

$80 $80 = **$2,000**

$3,000 CHALLENGE IN 26 WEEKS

Saving Purpose: _____

$75	$75	$75	$75
$75	$75	$100	$100
$100	$100	$100	$100
$125	$125	$125	$125
$125	$125	$150	$150
$150	$150	$150	$150

$150 + $150 = **$3,000**

$3,000 CHALLENGE IN 26 WEEKS

Saving Purpose: _____

$115	$115	$115	$115
$115	$115	$115	$115
$115	$115	$115	$115
$115	$115	$115	$115
$115	$115	$115	$115
$115	$115	$115	$115

$120 $120 = $3,000

$4,000 CHALLENGE IN 26 WEEKS

Saving Purpose: _____

$100	$110	$120	$130
$140	$150	$150	$150
$150	$150	$150	$150
$150	$150	$150	$150
$150	$160	$160	$170
$170	$180	$180	$190

$190 | $200 = **$4,000**

$4,000 CHALLENGE IN 26 WEEKS

Saving Purpose: _____

$150	$150	$150	$150
$150	$150	$155	$155
$155	$155	$155	$155
$155	$155	$155	$155
$155	$155	$155	$155
$155	$155	$155	$155

$155 | $155 | = $4,000

$5,000 CHALLENGE IN 26 WEEKS

Saving Purpose: _____

$55	$65	$75	$85
$95	$100	$105	$125
$125	$150	$160	$175
$185	$190	$200	$225
$235	$240	$250	$275
$275	$300	$315	$320
$325	$350	= $5,000

$5,000 CHALLENGE IN 26 WEEKS

Saving Purpose: _____

$190	$190	$190	$190
$190	$190	$190	$190
$190	$190	$190	$190
$190	$190	$195	$195
$195	$195	$195	$195
$195	$195	$195	$195
$195	$195

= $5,000

$10,000 CHALLENGE IN 26 WEEKS

Saving Purpose: _____

$90	$180	$190	$210
$270	$295	$330	$350
$350	$360	$365	$385
$385	$400	$425	$435
$450	$460	$480	$490
$500	$500	$510	$510

$525 | $555 = **$10,000**

$10,000 CHALLENGE IN 26 WEEKS

Saving Purpose: _____

$380	$380	$385	$385
$385	$385	$385	$385
$385	$385	$385	$385
$385	$385	$385	$385
$385	$385	$385	$385
$385	$385	$385	$385

$385 | $385 | = $10,000

$15,000 CHALLENGE IN 26 WEEKS

Saving Purpose: _____

$460	$470	$480	$490
$500	$500	$510	$520
$530	$540	$550	$560
$570	$580	$590	$600
$610	$620	$630	$640
$650	$660	$670	$680

$690 $700   = **$15,000**

$15,000 CHALLENGE IN 26 WEEKS

Saving Purpose: _____

$460	$470	$480	$490
$500	$500	$510	$520
$530	$540	$550	$560
$570	$580	$590	$600
$610	$620	$630	$640
$650	$660	$670	$680

$690 $700 = **$15,000**

CUSTOM CHALLENGE IN 26 WEEKS

Saving Purpose: _____

Total: _____

CUSTOM CHALLENGE IN 26 WEEKS

Saving Purpose: _____

Total: _____

$500 CHALLENGE IN 26 WEEKS

Saving Purpose: _____

$10	$10	$20	$20
$20	$20	$20	$20
$20	$20	$20	$20
$20	$20	$20	$20
$20	$20	$20	$20
$20	$20	$20	$20

$20 $20   = $500

$500 CHALLENGE IN 26 WEEKS

Saving Purpose: _____

$10	$10	$20	$20
$20	$20	$20	$20
$20	$20	$20	$20
$20	$20	$20	$20
$20	$20	$20	$20
$20	$20	$20	$20

$20 $20   **= $500**

$700 CHALLENGE IN 26 WEEKS

Saving Purpose: _____

$1	$2	$3	$4
$5	$6	$7	$8
$9	$10	$11	$12
$13	$14	$15	$16
$17	$18	$19	$20
$21	$22	$23	$24

$25 $26 = **$700**

$700 CHALLENGE IN 26 WEEKS

Saving Purpose: _____

$1	$2	$3	$4
$5	$6	$7	$8
$9	$10	$11	$12
$13	$14	$15	$16
$17	$18	$19	$20
$21	$22	$23	$24

$25 $26   = $700

$1,000 CHALLENGE IN 26 WEEKS

Saving Purpose: _____

$20	$20	$40	$40
$40	$40	$40	$40
$40	$40	$40	$40
$40	$40	$40	$40
$40	$40	$40	$40
$40	$40	$40	$40

$40 $40 = $1,000

$1,000 CHALLENGE IN 26 WEEKS

Saving Purpose: _____

$10	$15	$20	$20
$20	$25	$25	$25
$30	$30	$35	$35
$40	$40	$45	$45
$45	$50	$50	$50
$55	$55	$55	$60

$60 $60 = $1,000

$2,000 CHALLENGE IN 26 WEEKS

Saving Purpose: _____

$20	$30	$40	$40
$40	$50	$50	$50
$60	$60	$70	$70
$80	$80	$90	$90
$90	$100	$100	$100
$110	$110	$110	$120

$120 $120 = **$2,000**

$2,000 CHALLENGE IN 26 WEEKS

Saving Purpose: _____

$75	$75	$75	$75
$75	$75	$75	$75
$75	$75	$75	$75
$75	$75	$75	$75
$80	$80	$80	$80
$80	$80	$80	$80

$80 $80 = **$2,000**

$3,000 CHALLENGE IN 26 WEEKS

Saving Purpose: _____

$75	$75	$75	$75
$75	$75	$100	$100
$100	$100	$100	$100
$125	$125	$125	$125
$125	$125	$150	$150
$150	$150	$150	$150

$150 $150 = **$3,000**

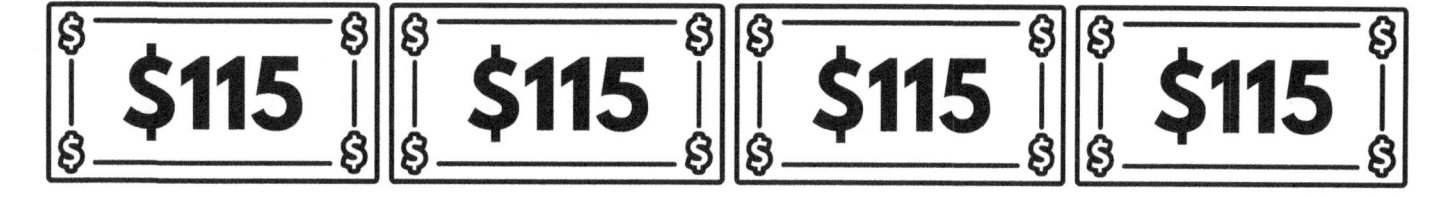

$3,000 CHALLENGE IN 26 WEEKS

Saving Purpose: _____

$115	$115	$115	$115
$115	$115	$115	$115
$115	$115	$115	$115
$115	$115	$115	$115
$115	$115	$115	$115
$115	$115	$115	$115

$120 + $120 = **$3,000**

$4,000 CHALLENGE IN 26 WEEKS

Saving Purpose: _____

$100	$110	$120	$130
$140	$150	$150	$150
$150	$150	$150	$150
$150	$150	$150	$150
$150	$160	$160	$170
$170	$180	$180	$190

$190 | $200 = $4,000

$4,000 CHALLENGE IN 26 WEEKS

Saving Purpose: _____

$150	$150	$150	$150
$150	$150	$155	$155
$155	$155	$155	$155
$155	$155	$155	$155
$155	$155	$155	$155
$155	$155	$155	$155

$155 $155 = **$4,000**

$5,000 CHALLENGE IN 26 WEEKS

Saving Purpose: _____

$55	$65	$75	$85
$95	$100	$105	$125
$125	$150	$160	$175
$185	$190	$200	$225
$235	$240	$250	$275
$275	$300	$315	$320

$325 + $350 = **$5,000**

$5,000 CHALLENGE IN 26 WEEKS

Saving Purpose: _____

$190	$190	$190	$190
$190	$190	$190	$190
$190	$190	$190	$190
$190	$190	$195	$195
$195	$195	$195	$195
$195	$195	$195	$195

$195 $195 = **$5,000**

$10,000 CHALLENGE IN 26 WEEKS

Saving Purpose: _____

$90	$180	$190	$210
$270	$295	$330	$350
$350	$360	$365	$385
$385	$400	$425	$435
$450	$460	$480	$490
$500	$500	$510	$510
$525	$555		

= $10,000

$10,000 CHALLENGE IN 26 WEEKS

Saving Purpose: _____

$380	$380	$385	$385
$385	$385	$385	$385
$385	$385	$385	$385
$385	$385	$385	$385
$385	$385	$385	$385
$385	$385	$385	$385

$385 $385 = $10,000

$15,000 CHALLENGE IN 26 WEEKS

Saving Purpose: _____

$460	$470	$480	$490
$500	$500	$510	$520
$530	$540	$550	$560
$570	$580	$590	$600
$610	$620	$630	$640
$650	$660	$670	$680

$690 $700   = **$15,000**

$15,000 CHALLENGE IN 26 WEEKS

Saving Purpose: _____

$460	$470	$480	$490
$500	$500	$510	$520
$530	$540	$550	$560
$570	$580	$590	$600
$610	$620	$630	$640
$650	$660	$670	$680

$690 | $700 | = $15,000

CUSTOM CHALLENGE IN 26 WEEKS

Saving Purpose: _____

Total: _____

CUSTOM CHALLENGE IN 26 WEEKS

Saving Purpose: _____

Total: _____

$500 CHALLENGE IN 26 WEEKS

Saving Purpose: _____

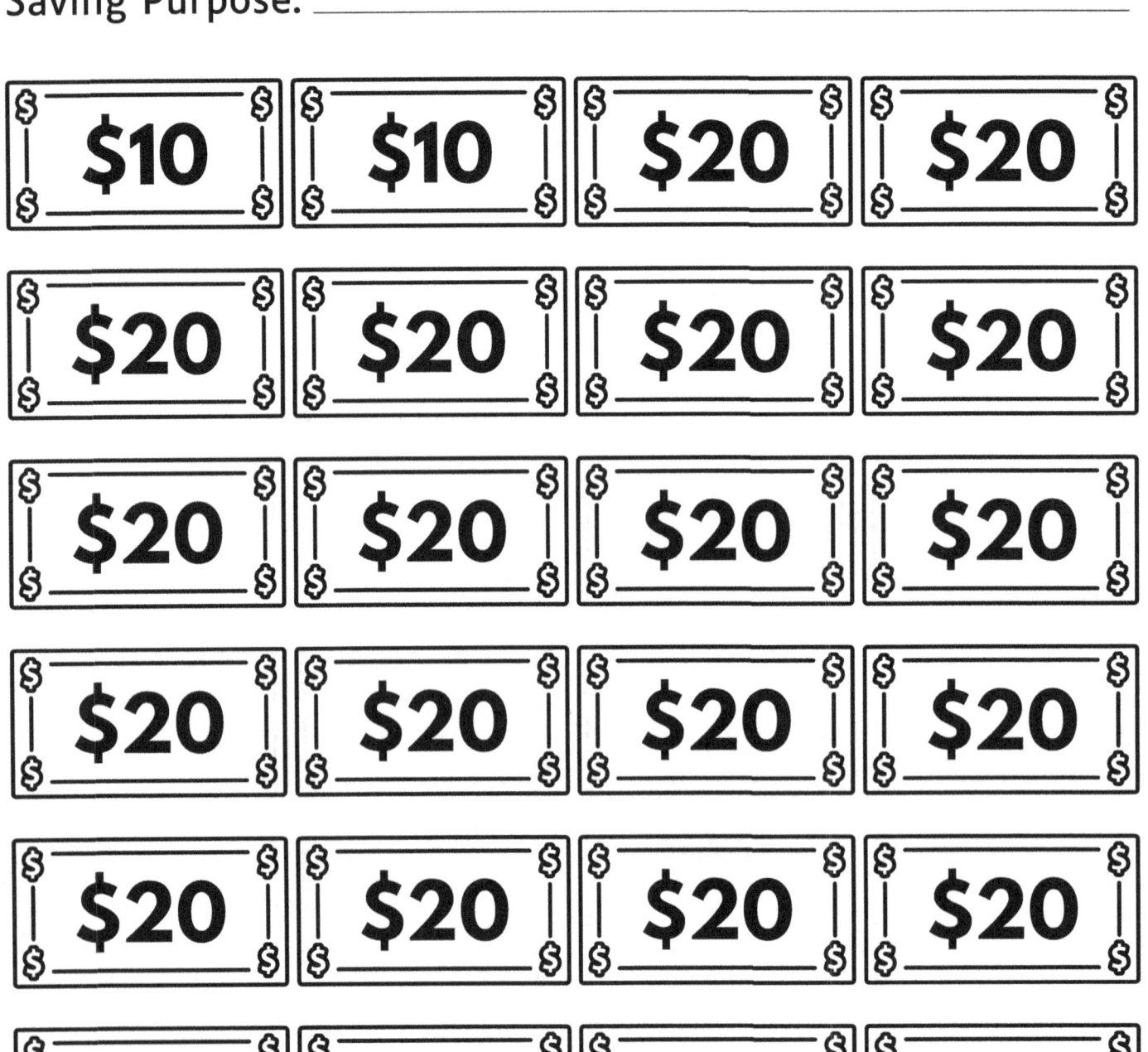

$10	$10	$20	$20
$20	$20	$20	$20
$20	$20	$20	$20
$20	$20	$20	$20
$20	$20	$20	$20
$20	$20	$20	$20

$20 $20 **= $500**

$500 CHALLENGE IN 26 WEEKS

Saving Purpose: _____

$10	$10	$20	$20
$20	$20	$20	$20
$20	$20	$20	$20
$20	$20	$20	$20
$20	$20	$20	$20
$20	$20	$20	$20

$20 $20 = **$500**

$700 CHALLENGE IN 26 WEEKS

Saving Purpose: _____

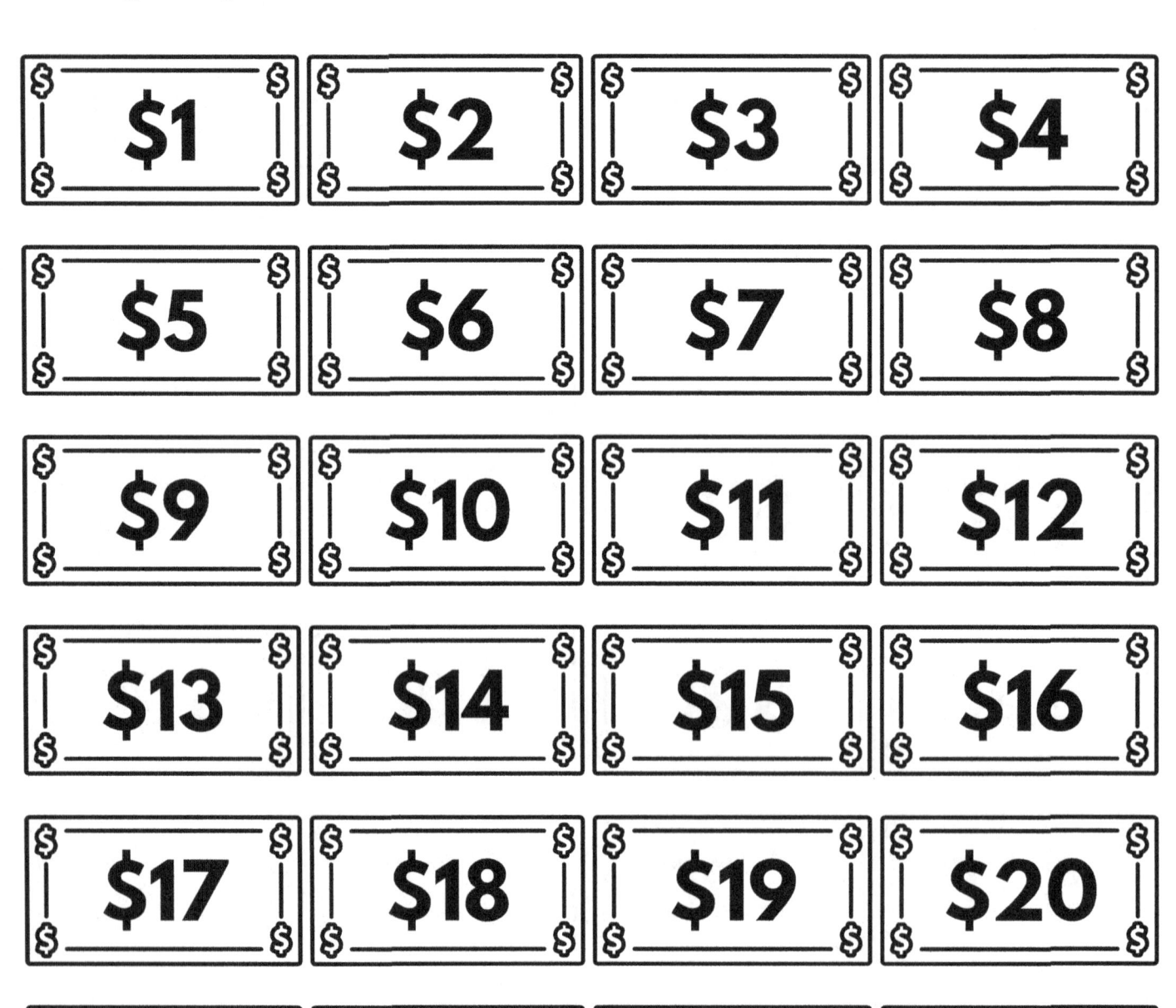

$1	$2	$3	$4
$5	$6	$7	$8
$9	$10	$11	$12
$13	$14	$15	$16
$17	$18	$19	$20
$21	$22	$23	$24

$25 $26 = **$700**

$700 CHALLENGE IN 26 WEEKS

Saving Purpose: _____

$1	$2	$3	$4
$5	$6	$7	$8
$9	$10	$11	$12
$13	$14	$15	$16
$17	$18	$19	$20
$21	$22	$23	$24

$25 $26 = **$700**

$1,000 CHALLENGE IN 26 WEEKS

Saving Purpose: _____

$20	$20	$40	$40
$40	$40	$40	$40
$40	$40	$40	$40
$40	$40	$40	$40
$40	$40	$40	$40
$40	$40	$40	$40

$40 $40   = **$1,000**

$1,000 CHALLENGE IN 26 WEEKS

Saving Purpose: _____

$10	$15	$20	$20
$20	$25	$25	$25
$30	$30	$35	$35
$40	$40	$45	$45
$45	$50	$50	$50
$55	$55	$55	$60
$60	$60

= $1,000

$2,000 CHALLENGE IN 26 WEEKS

Saving Purpose: _____

$20	$30	$40	$40
$40	$50	$50	$50
$60	$60	$70	$70
$80	$80	$90	$90
$90	$100	$100	$100
$110	$110	$110	$120

$120 $120 = **$2,000**

$2,000 CHALLENGE IN 26 WEEKS

Saving Purpose: _____

$75	$75	$75	$75
$75	$75	$75	$75
$75	$75	$75	$75
$75	$75	$75	$75
$80	$80	$80	$80
$80	$80	$80	$80

$80 $80 = **$2,000**

$3,000 CHALLENGE IN 26 WEEKS

Saving Purpose: _____

$75	$75	$75	$75
$75	$75	$100	$100
$100	$100	$100	$100
$125	$125	$125	$125
$125	$125	$150	$150
$150	$150	$150	$150
$150	$150	= $3,000

$3,000 CHALLENGE IN 26 WEEKS

Saving Purpose: _____

$115	$115	$115	$115
$115	$115	$115	$115
$115	$115	$115	$115
$115	$115	$115	$115
$115	$115	$115	$115
$115	$115	$115	$115

$120 + $120 = **$3,000**

$4,000 CHALLENGE IN 26 WEEKS

Saving Purpose: _____

$100	$110	$120	$130
$140	$150	$150	$150
$150	$150	$150	$150
$150	$150	$150	$150
$150	$160	$160	$170
$170	$180	$180	$190

$190 $200 = **$4,000**

$4,000 CHALLENGE IN 26 WEEKS

Saving Purpose: _____

$150	$150	$150	$150
$150	$150	$155	$155
$155	$155	$155	$155
$155	$155	$155	$155
$155	$155	$155	$155
$155	$155	$155	$155

$155 $155 **= $4,000**

$5,000 CHALLENGE IN 26 WEEKS

Saving Purpose: _____

$55	$65	$75	$85
$95	$100	$105	$125
$125	$150	$160	$175
$185	$190	$200	$225
$235	$240	$250	$275
$275	$300	$315	$320

$325 | $350 | = $5,000

$5,000 CHALLENGE IN 26 WEEKS

Saving Purpose: _____

$190	$190	$190	$190
$190	$190	$190	$190
$190	$190	$190	$190
$190	$190	$195	$195
$195	$195	$195	$195
$195	$195	$195	$195

$195 | $195 | = **$5,000**

$10,000 CHALLENGE IN 26 WEEKS

Saving Purpose: _____

$90	$180	$190	$210
$270	$295	$330	$350
$350	$360	$365	$385
$385	$400	$425	$435
$450	$460	$480	$490
$500	$500	$510	$510

$525 $555 = $10,000

$10,000 CHALLENGE IN 26 WEEKS

Saving Purpose: _____

$380	$380	$385	$385
$385	$385	$385	$385
$385	$385	$385	$385
$385	$385	$385	$385
$385	$385	$385	$385
$385	$385	$385	$385

$385 $385 = **$10,000**

$15,000 CHALLENGE IN 26 WEEKS

Saving Purpose: _____

$460	$470	$480	$490
$500	$500	$510	$520
$530	$540	$550	$560
$570	$580	$590	$600
$610	$620	$630	$640
$650	$660	$670	$680

$690 $700 = **$15,000**

$15,000 CHALLENGE IN 26 WEEKS

Saving Purpose: _____

$460	$470	$480	$490
$500	$500	$510	$520
$530	$540	$550	$560
$570	$580	$590	$600
$610	$620	$630	$640
$650	$660	$670	$680

$690 $700 = $15,000

CUSTOM CHALLENGE IN 26 WEEKS

Saving Purpose: _____

Total: _____

CUSTOM CHALLENGE IN 26 WEEKS

Saving Purpose: _____

Total: _____

$500 CHALLENGE IN 26 WEEKS

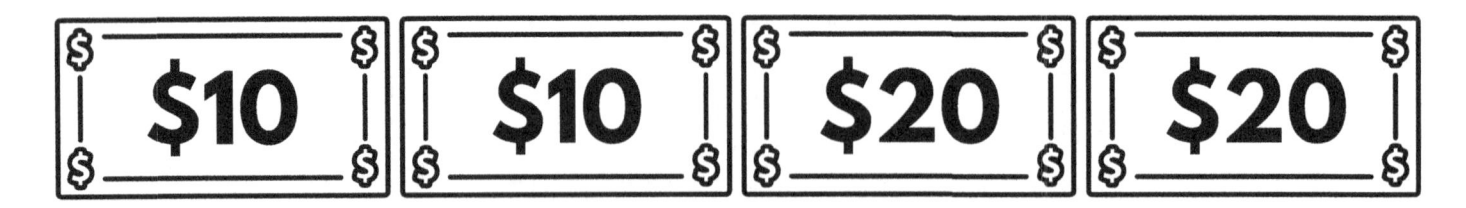

Saving Purpose: _____

$10	$10	$20	$20
$20	$20	$20	$20
$20	$20	$20	$20
$20	$20	$20	$20
$20	$20	$20	$20
$20	$20	$20	$20

$20 $20 = $500

$500 CHALLENGE IN 26 WEEKS

Saving Purpose: _____

$10	$10	$20	$20
$20	$20	$20	$20
$20	$20	$20	$20
$20	$20	$20	$20
$20	$20	$20	$20
$20	$20	$20	$20

$20 $20 = **$500**

$700 CHALLENGE IN 26 WEEKS

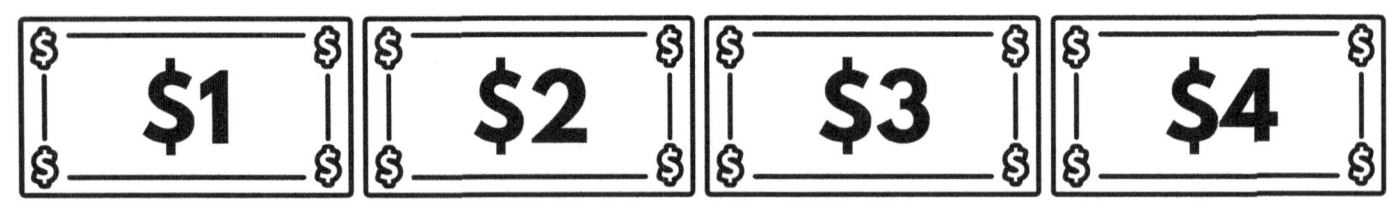

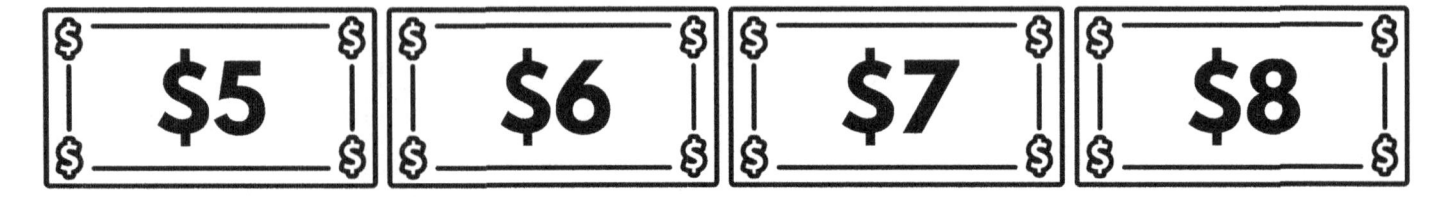

Saving Purpose: _____

$1	$2	$3	$4
$5	$6	$7	$8
$9	$10	$11	$12
$13	$14	$15	$16
$17	$18	$19	$20
$21	$22	$23	$24

$25 $26 = **$700**

$700 CHALLENGE IN 26 WEEKS

Saving Purpose: _____

$1	$2	$3	$4
$5	$6	$7	$8
$9	$10	$11	$12
$13	$14	$15	$16
$17	$18	$19	$20
$21	$22	$23	$24

$25 $26 = **$700**

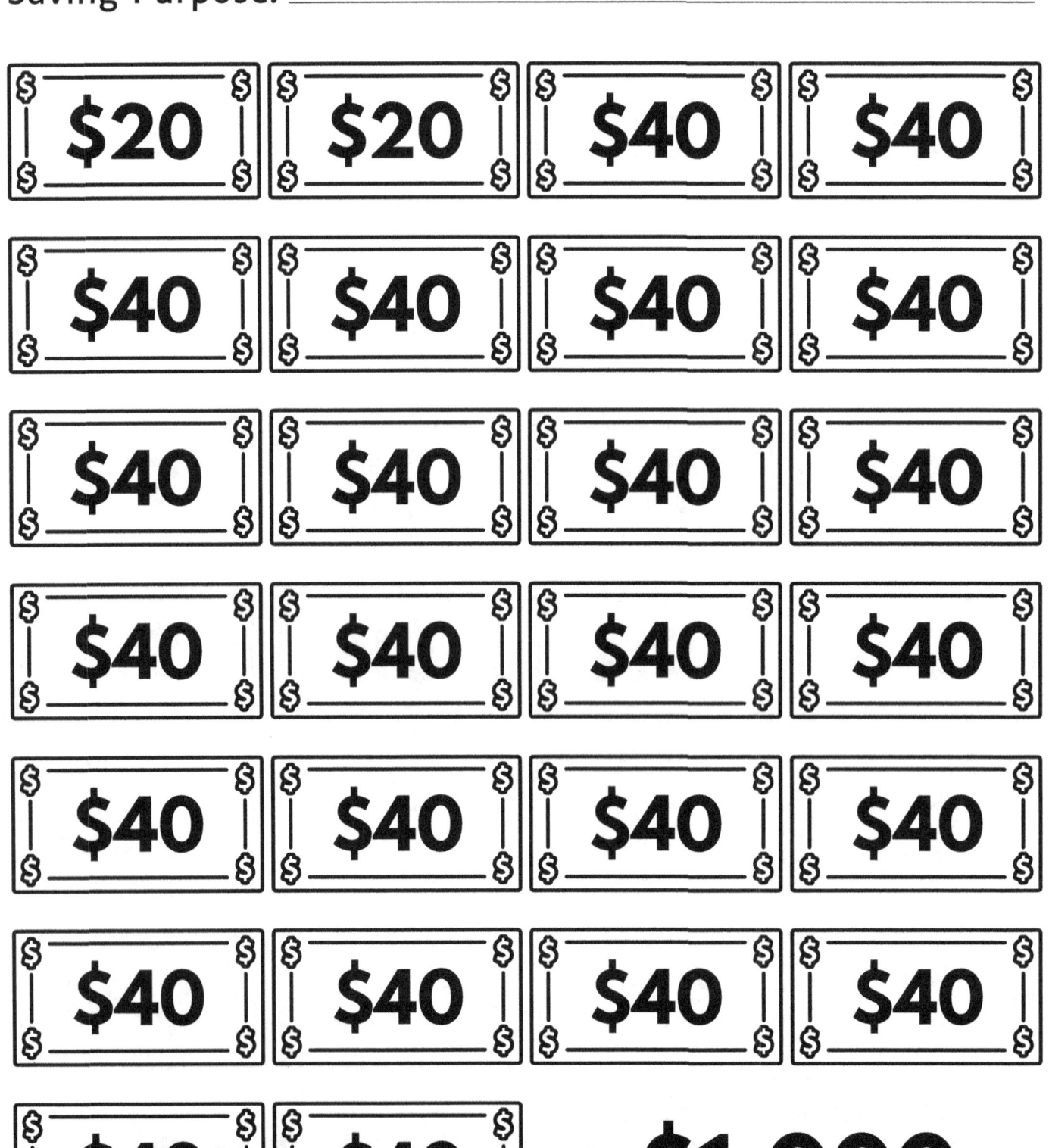

$1,000 CHALLENGE IN 26 WEEKS

Saving Purpose: _____

$20	$20	$40	$40
$40	$40	$40	$40
$40	$40	$40	$40
$40	$40	$40	$40
$40	$40	$40	$40
$40	$40	$40	$40

$40 $40 = **$1,000**

$1,000 CHALLENGE IN 26 WEEKS

Saving Purpose: _____

$10	$15	$20	$20
$20	$25	$25	$25
$30	$30	$35	$35
$40	$40	$45	$45
$45	$50	$50	$50
$55	$55	$55	$60
$60	$60		

= $1,000

$2,000 CHALLENGE IN 26 WEEKS

Saving Purpose: _____

$20	$30	$40	$40
$40	$50	$50	$50
$60	$60	$70	$70
$80	$80	$90	$90
$90	$100	$100	$100
$110	$110	$110	$120

$120 $120   = $2,000

$2,000 CHALLENGE IN 26 WEEKS

Saving Purpose: _____

$75	$75	$75	$75
$75	$75	$75	$75
$75	$75	$75	$75
$75	$75	$75	$75
$80	$80	$80	$80
$80	$80	$80	$80

$80 $80 **= $2,000**

$3,000 CHALLENGE IN 26 WEEKS

Saving Purpose: _____

$75	$75	$75	$75
$75	$75	$100	$100
$100	$100	$100	$100
$125	$125	$125	$125
$125	$125	$150	$150
$150	$150	$150	$150

$150 $150 = **$3,000**

$3,000 CHALLENGE IN 26 WEEKS

Saving Purpose: _____

$115	$115	$115	$115
$115	$115	$115	$115
$115	$115	$115	$115
$115	$115	$115	$115
$115	$115	$115	$115
$115	$115	$115	$115

$120 $120 = **$3,000**

$4,000 CHALLENGE IN 26 WEEKS

Saving Purpose: _____

$100	$110	$120	$130
$140	$150	$150	$150
$150	$150	$150	$150
$150	$150	$150	$150
$150	$160	$160	$170
$170	$180	$180	$190
$190	$200		

$190 + $200 = **$4,000**

$4,000 CHALLENGE IN 26 WEEKS

Saving Purpose: _____

$150	$150	$150	$150
$150	$150	$155	$155
$155	$155	$155	$155
$155	$155	$155	$155
$155	$155	$155	$155
$155	$155	$155	$155

$155 $155 = $4,000

$5,000 CHALLENGE IN 26 WEEKS

Saving Purpose: _____

$55	$65	$75	$85
$95	$100	$105	$125
$125	$150	$160	$175
$185	$190	$200	$225
$235	$240	$250	$275
$275	$300	$315	$320

$325 $350 = **$5,000**

$5,000 CHALLENGE IN 26 WEEKS

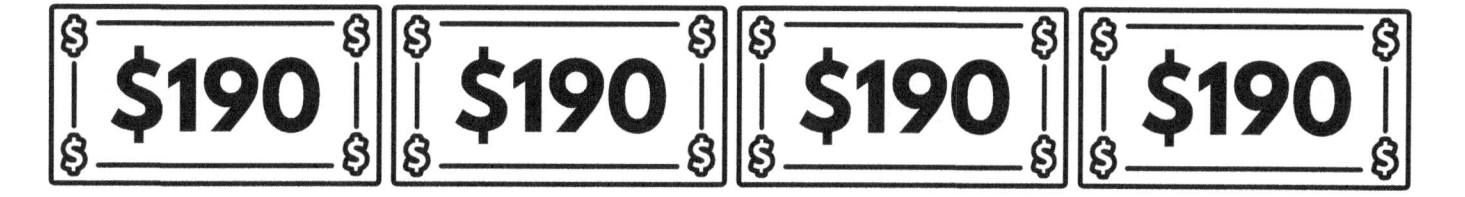

Saving Purpose: _____

$190	$190	$190	$190
$190	$190	$190	$190
$190	$190	$190	$190
$190	$190	$195	$195
$195	$195	$195	$195
$195	$195	$195	$195

$195 $195 = $5,000

$10,000 CHALLENGE IN 26 WEEKS

Saving Purpose: _____

$90	$180	$190	$210
$270	$295	$330	$350
$350	$360	$365	$385
$385	$400	$425	$435
$450	$460	$480	$490
$500	$500	$510	$510

$525 + $555 = **$10,000**

$10,000 CHALLENGE IN 26 WEEKS

Saving Purpose: _____

$380	$380	$385	$385
$385	$385	$385	$385
$385	$385	$385	$385
$385	$385	$385	$385
$385	$385	$385	$385
$385	$385	$385	$385

$385 $385 **= $10,000**

$15,000 CHALLENGE IN 26 WEEKS

Saving Purpose: _____

$460	$470	$480	$490
$500	$500	$510	$520
$530	$540	$550	$560
$570	$580	$590	$600
$610	$620	$630	$640
$650	$660	$670	$680

$690 $700   = $15,000

$15,000 CHALLENGE IN 26 WEEKS

Saving Purpose: _____

$460	$470	$480	$490
$500	$500	$510	$520
$530	$540	$550	$560
$570	$580	$590	$600
$610	$620	$630	$640
$650	$660	$670	$680

$690 $700 **= $15,000**

CUSTOM CHALLENGE IN 26 WEEKS

Saving Purpose: _____

Total: _____

Made in United States
North Haven, CT
11 November 2022